To My Wonderful Mother
Meine Kleine Mutti

———— ✒ ————

This allegory is about your journey as a mother.
As your children grow to adulthood, the hope is that
they will choose the way of wisdom.
But you cannot make their choices—you can only choose to be
faithful to God and faithful to your children.

My thanks to all the wonderful people at WaterBrook Press
for appreciating the message of *A Mother's Journey*,
and to Wendy Reis for her beautiful design.

The idea for *A Mother's Journey* came from an old selection
about a mother quoted in *Streams in the Desert Volume II*
by Mrs. Charles E. Cowman, attributed to Temple Bailey,
from *Food for Thought*.

A MOTHER'S JOURNEY
PUBLISHED BY WATERBROOK PRESS
5446 North Academy Boulevard, Suite 200
Colorado Springs, Colorado 80918
A division of Random House, Inc.

ISBN 1-57856-041-1
© 1997 by Linda Dillow
Illustrations © 1997 by Joel Spector

A Mother's Journey

LINDA DILLOW

WATERBROOK
PRESS

The young mother grasped
the hands of her children and looked
at the path before her.

"Is the way long?" she asked.

And her Shepherd answered,
*"Yes,
and the way is hard,
and you will be old before you reach
the end of it.
But the end will be better
than the beginning."*

"*What is required?*" asked the mother.
And her Shepherd replied,

Faithfulness

Give Me your hopes,
give Me your dreams;
The journey is long
and not what it seems.
Affirm your children,
be faithful to Me;
This is the Mother
I want you to be.

Springtime

It was spring. The trees burst with blossoms. Cheerful wildflowers covered the fields, and a bubbling brook echoed peals of laughter as it meandered through the meadow.

Like little lambs the children frolicked, following the mother through sweet−smelling clover along the path.

The days were good, the evenings peaceful.

The young mother was happy as she played with her children. Together they made daisy chains from the gathered wildflowers, and bathed in clear streams.

The sun shone on their path, and life was sweet.
The young mother cried,

"Nothing will ever be lovelier than this!

I have given
my children joy!

And her Shepherd said,

You were faithful in the good times

Give Me your hopes,
give Me your dreams;
The journey is long
and not what it seems.
Affirm your children,
be faithful to Me;
This is the Mother
I want you to be.

The children grew like sunflowers dancing along the hillside. The days were long. But the air was thick.

A summer storm rolled across the heavens. Lightning flashed, hail pounded, and the children shook with cold and fear.

The path was steep and the children grew weary. But the mother encircled them with the warmth of her love. "Walk on, dear ones," she said. "We will soon be there."

So the children climbed.

When they finally ascended above the storm, they said, "We could not have made it without you, Mother."

Summertime

And she rejoiced.

"This is better than the joy
of Springtime, for...

I have taught my children perseverance

And her Shepherd said,

You were faithful in the hard times

Give Me your hopes,
give Me your dreams;
The journey is long
and not what it seems.
Affirm your children,
be faithful to Me;
This is the Mother
I want you to be.

Autumn

Golden aspen leaves drifted to the ground, but the trees stood tall in the Autumn breeze.

And the children shed the leaves of childhood.

Multicolored winds of doubt and temptation whipped around their teenage hearts, and they chased foolish fantasies along the path.

The mother's heart feared. She saw the many hidden traps that lay before them.

At times the journey was painful and the mother faltered.

As the Shepherd gave her counsel, the mother tried skillfully to lead her children around the snares.

And at Autumn's end the mother said,

"This season is better than Summer or Spring,
for in Autumn

I taught my children wisdom

And her Shepherd said,

You were faithful when your heart was breaking

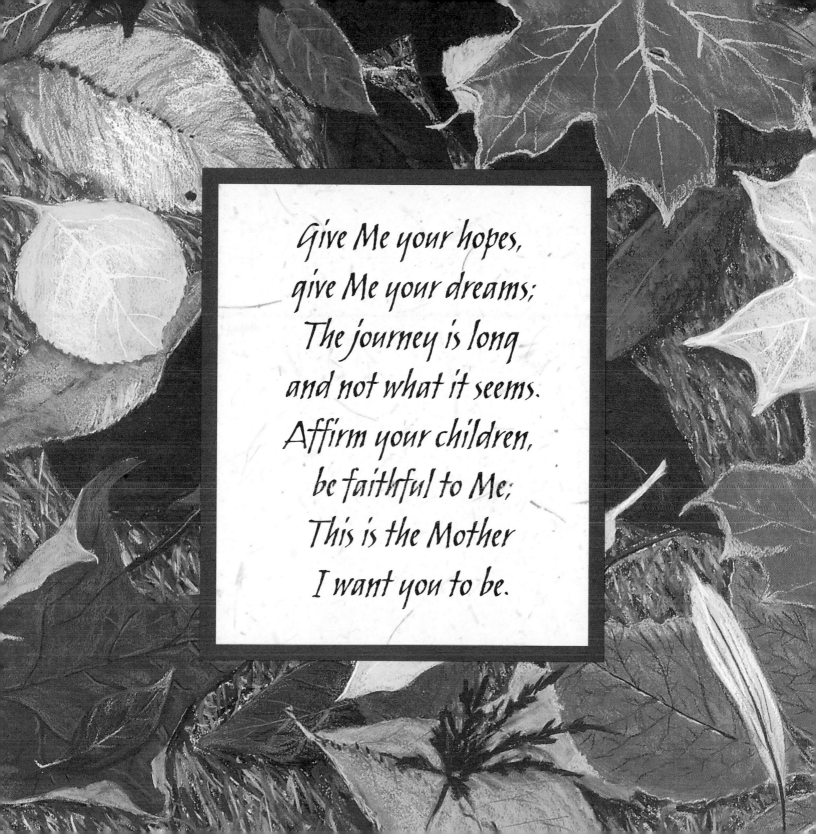

Give Me your hopes,
give Me your dreams;
The journey is long
and not what it seems.
Affirm your children,
be faithful to Me;
This is the Mother
I want you to be.

Mountain snow weighted the limbs
of the stately pine trees. Like them,
the young adults stood tall.

In the night of Winter, threatening
clouds of prejudice, oppression,
and disease darkened the earth.
The world had turned inside out.

Sometimes the young adults groped
and stumbled. "Look up," their
mother said. "Lift your eyes
to the Light of Life."

Above the clouds they saw the One
who brings Light out of darkness.
He grasped their hands
and gave them peace.

Winter

As the snow slipped off
the pine boughs, the mother said,

"*Winter is the best season of all, for...*

I have shown my children God

And her Shepherd said,

You were
faithful to give
your children
to Me

Give Me your hopes,
give Me your dreams;
The journey is long
and not what it seems.
Affirm your children,
be faithful to Me;
This is the Mother
I want you to be.

The seasons marched on
and the mother grew old.
She was frail and bent.

But her children were tall and strong,
and walked in the way of wisdom.

When the journey was hard,
they helped their mother.

When the path was rough,
they lifted her.

At last they came to the pinnacle of the highest mountain.

Beyond it they saw a shining road and a golden gate flung wide.

There stood the brilliant tree of life.

The mother said, "I have reached the end of my journey. I have been faithful to my children and faithful to God. The end is better than the beginning, for...

My children can walk alone with the Shepherd

As she passed through the gates,
she heard her Shepherd say,

Well Done

You gave Me your hopes,
gave Me your dreams;
Though the path of life
was not what it seemed.
You affirmed your children,
were faithful to Me;
You were the Mother
I asked you to be.

She heard her children calling,
"You will always walk with us, Mother!"

They stood and watched as the gates closed after her.
And she heard her children saying,

A faithful mother is more than a memory;

a faithful mother lives with us forever.

And her children grasped the hands
of their own children and looked
at the path before them.

"Is the way long?" they asked.

And their Shepherd answered,
"Yes,
and the way is hard,
and you will be old before you reach
the end of it...

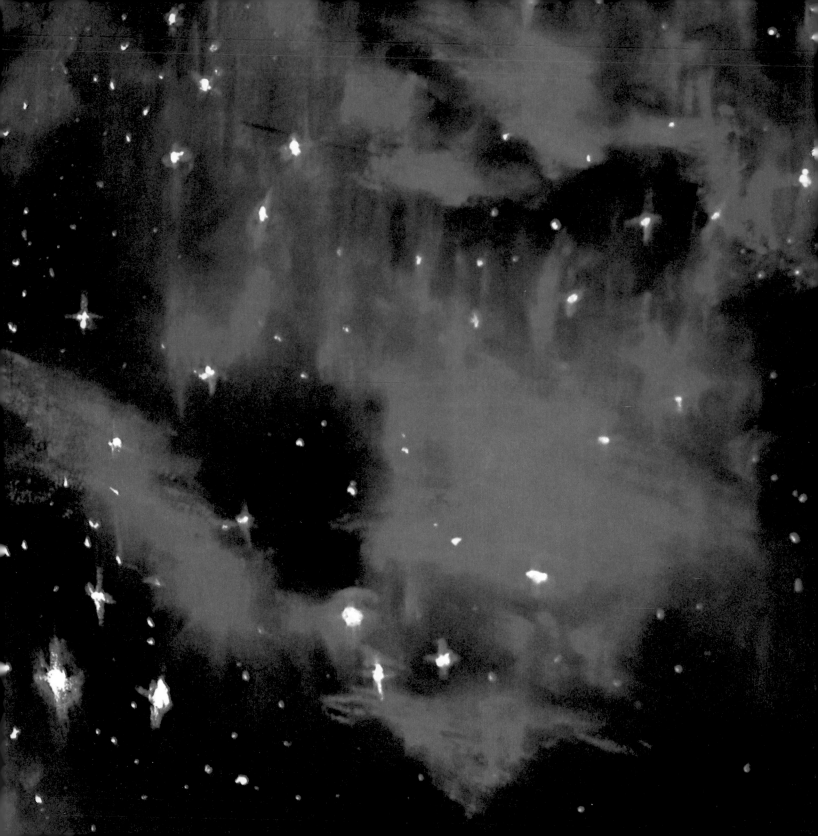

But the end
will be better
than the
beginning